Rupert Bear

DIARY 2016

First published in 2015

15 17 19 18 16
1 3 5 7 9 10 8 6 4 2

Created and produced by
FLAME TREE PUBLISHING

6 Melbray Mews,
London SW6 3NS, UK
Tel: +44 (0) 20 7751 9650
Fax: +44 (0) 20 7751 9651
info@flametreepublishing.com
www.flametreepublishing.com

www.flametreepublishing.com

ISBN 978-1-78361-553-7

© Flame Tree Publishing Ltd.

A CIP record for this book is available from the British Library upon request.

All rights reserved. No part of this publication may be reproduced, stored in a retrieval system,
or transmitted in any form or by any means, electronic, mechanical, photocopying,
recording or otherwise, without the prior permission in writing of the publisher.

Every attempt has been made to ensure the accuracy of the date information at the time of going
to press, and the publishers cannot accept responsibility for any errors. Some public holidays are subject
to change by Royal or State proclamation. At the time of publication, accurate information was unavailable
for all religious celebrations in 2016. All Jewish and Islamic holidays begin at sunset on the previous
day and end at sunset on the date shown.

Every effort has been made to contact all copyright holders. The publishers
would be pleased to hear if any oversights or omissions have occurred.

Rupert Bear™ & © 2015 Classic Media Distribution Limited & Express Newspapers.

Printed in China

JANUARY	FEBRUARY	MARCH	APRIL	MAY
M T W T F S S	M T W T F S S	M T W T F S S	M T W T F S S	M T W T F S S
1 2 3 4 5 6 7 8 9 10 11 12 13 14 15 16 17 18 19 20 21 22 23 24 25 26 27 28 29 30 31	1 2 3 4 5 6 7 8 9 10 11 12 13 14 15 16 17 18 19 20 21 22 23 24 25 26 27 28	1 2 3 4 5 6 7 8 9 10 11 12 13 14 15 16 17 18 19 20 21 22 23 24 25 26 27 28 29 30 31	1 2 3 4 5 6 7 8 9 10 11 12 13 14 15 16 17 18 19 20 21 22 23 24 25 26 27 28 29 30	1 2 3 4 5 6 7 8 9 10 11 12 13 14 15 16 17 18 19 20 21 22 23 24 25 26 27 28 29 30 31

JUNE			JULY
M T W T F S S			M T W T F S S
1 2 3 4 5 6 7 8 9 10 11 12 13 14 15 16 17 18 19 20 21 22 23 24 25 26 27 28 29 30		2015	1 2 3 4 5 6 7 8 9 10 11 12 13 14 15 16 17 18 19 20 21 22 23 24 25 26 27 28 29 30 31

AUGUST	SEPTEMBER	OCTOBER	NOVEMBER	DECEMBER
M T W T F S S	M T W T F S S	M T W T F S S	M T W T F S S	M T W T F S S
1 2 3 4 5 6 7 8 9 10 11 12 13 14 15 16 17 18 19 20 21 22 23 24 25 26 27 28 29 30 31	1 2 3 4 5 6 7 8 9 10 11 12 13 14 15 16 17 18 19 20 21 22 23 24 25 26 27 28 29 30	1 2 3 4 5 6 7 8 9 10 11 12 13 14 15 16 17 18 19 20 21 22 23 24 25 26 27 28 29 30 31	1 2 3 4 5 6 7 8 9 10 11 12 13 14 15 16 17 18 19 20 21 22 23 24 25 26 27 28 29 30	1 2 3 4 5 6 7 8 9 10 11 12 13 14 15 16 17 18 19 20 21 22 23 24 25 26 27 28 29 30 31

JANUARY	FEBRUARY	MARCH	APRIL	MAY
M T W T F S S	M T W T F S S	M T W T F S S	M T W T F S S	M T W T F S S
1 2 3 4 5 6 7 8 9 10 11 12 13 14 15 16 17 18 19 20 21 22 23 24 25 26 27 28 29 30 31	1 2 3 4 5 6 7 8 9 10 11 12 13 14 15 16 17 18 19 20 21 22 23 24 25 26 27 28	1 2 3 4 5 6 7 8 9 10 11 12 13 14 15 16 17 18 19 20 21 22 23 24 25 26 27 28 29 30 31	1 2 3 4 5 6 7 8 9 10 11 12 13 14 15 16 17 18 19 20 21 22 23 24 25 26 27 28 29 30	1 2 3 4 5 6 7 8 9 10 11 12 13 14 15 16 17 18 19 20 21 22 23 24 25 26 27 28 29 30 31

JUNE			JULY
M T W T F S S			M T W T F S S
1 2 3 4 5 6 7 8 9 10 11 12 13 14 15 16 17 18 19 20 21 22 23 24 25 26 27 28 29 30		2017 	1 2 3 4 5 6 7 8 9 10 11 12 13 14 15 16 17 18 19 20 21 22 23 24 25 26 27 28 29 30 31

AUGUST	SEPTEMBER	OCTOBER	NOVEMBER	DECEMBER
M T W T F S S	M T W T F S S	M T W T F S S	M T W T F S S	M T W T F S S
1 2 3 4 5 6 7 8 9 10 11 12 13 14 15 16 17 18 19 20 21 22 23 24 25 26 27 28 29 30 31	1 2 3 4 5 6 7 8 9 10 11 12 13 14 15 16 17 18 19 20 21 22 23 24 25 26 27 28 29 30	1 2 3 4 5 6 7 8 9 10 11 12 13 14 15 16 17 18 19 20 21 22 23 24 25 26 27 28 29 30 31	1 2 3 4 5 6 7 8 9 10 11 12 13 14 15 16 17 18 19 20 21 22 23 24 25 26 27 28 29 30	1 2 3 4 5 6 7 8 9 10 11 12 13 14 15 16 17 18 19 20 21 22 23 24 25 26 27 28 29 30 31

1960 endpaper

Personal Information

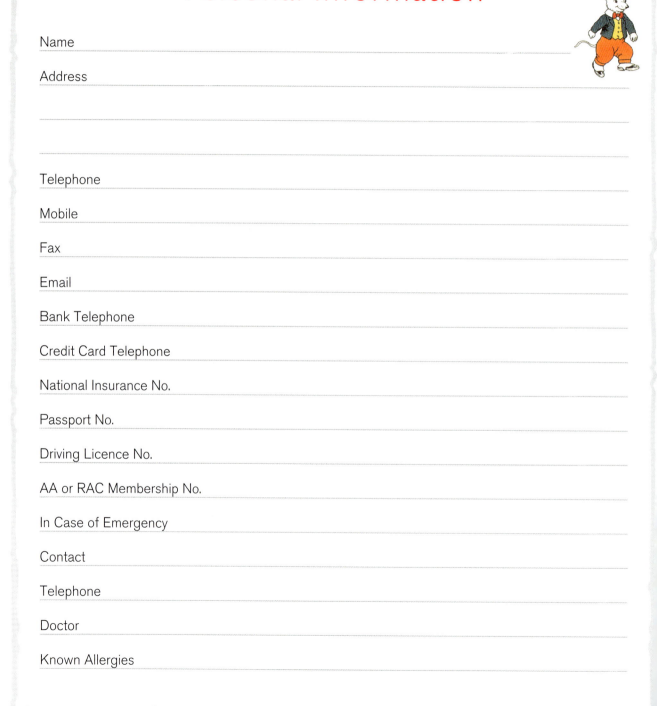

Name

Address

Telephone

Mobile

Fax

Email

Bank Telephone

Credit Card Telephone

National Insurance No.

Passport No.

Driving Licence No.

AA or RAC Membership No.

In Case of Emergency

Contact

Telephone

Doctor

Known Allergies

Notes

December 2015/January

WEEK 1

28 Monday

Boxing Day (observed)

29 Tuesday

30 Wednesday

31 Thursday

New Year's Eve

1 Friday

New Year's Day

2 Saturday

Public Holiday (Scot, NZ)

3 Sunday

WEEK 2

January

4 Monday

Public Holiday (Scot, NZ) (observed)

5 Tuesday

Birthday of Guru Gobind Singh

6 Wednesday

Epiphany
Three Kings' Day

7 Thursday

8 Friday

9 Saturday

10 Sunday

WEEK 3

January

11 Monday

Coming of Age Day (Japan)

12 Tuesday

13 Wednesday

14 Thursday

Makar Sakranti

15 Friday

16 Saturday

17 Sunday

Page 2 of the 1949 annual

January

WEEK 4

18 Monday

Martin Luther King Jr Day (USA)

19 Tuesday

20 Wednesday

21 Thursday

22 Friday

23 Saturday

24 Sunday

Page 2 of the 1950 annual

January

WEEK 5

25 Monday

Burns Night (Scot)

26 Tuesday

Australia Day

27 Wednesday

28 Thursday

29 Friday

30 Saturday

31 Sunday

WEEK 6

February

1 Monday

2 Tuesday

Groundhog Day (USA, Can)

3 Wednesday

4 Thursday

5 Friday

6 Saturday

Waitangi Day (NZ)

7 Sunday

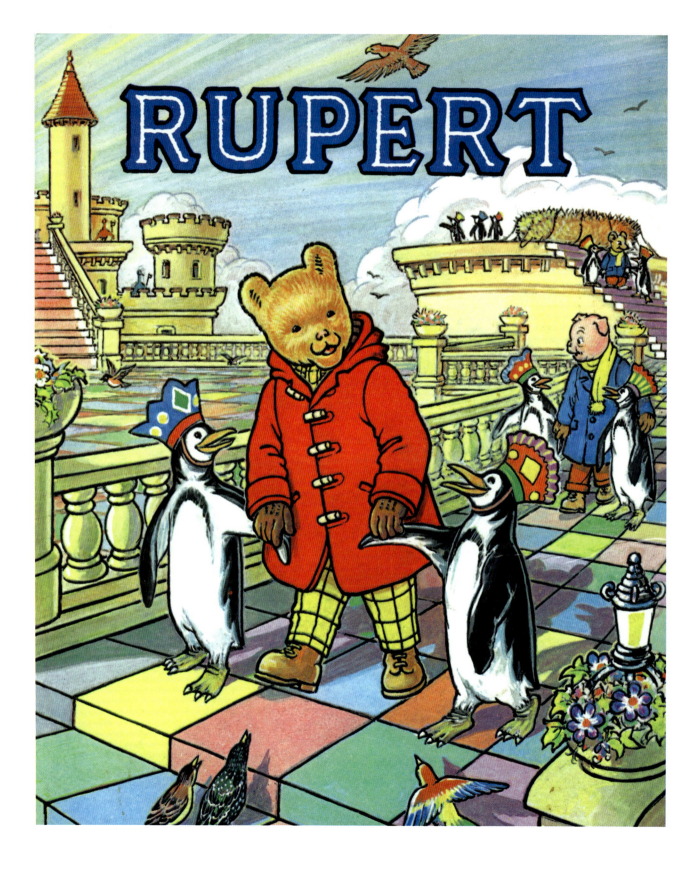

WEEK 7   February

8 Monday

Waitangi Day (NZ) (observed)
Chinese New Year
Year of the Monkey

9 Tuesday

Shrove Tuesday
Pancake Day

10 Wednesday

Ash Wednesday

11 Thursday

National Foundation Day (Japan)

12 Friday

Vasant Panchami

13 Saturday

14 Sunday

St Valentine's Day
First Sunday of Lent

Cover of the 1977 annual

February

WEEK 8

15 Monday

Presidents' Day (USA)

16 Tuesday

17 Wednesday

18 Thursday

19 Friday

20 Saturday

21 Sunday

Page 115 of the 1963 annual

February

WEEK 9

22 Monday

23 Tuesday

24 Wednesday

25 Thursday

26 Friday

27 Saturday

28 Sunday

WEEK 10

February/March

29 Monday

1 Tuesday

St David's Day (Wales)

2 Wednesday

3 Thursday

4 Friday

5 Saturday

6 Sunday

Mothering Sunday (UK, Eire)

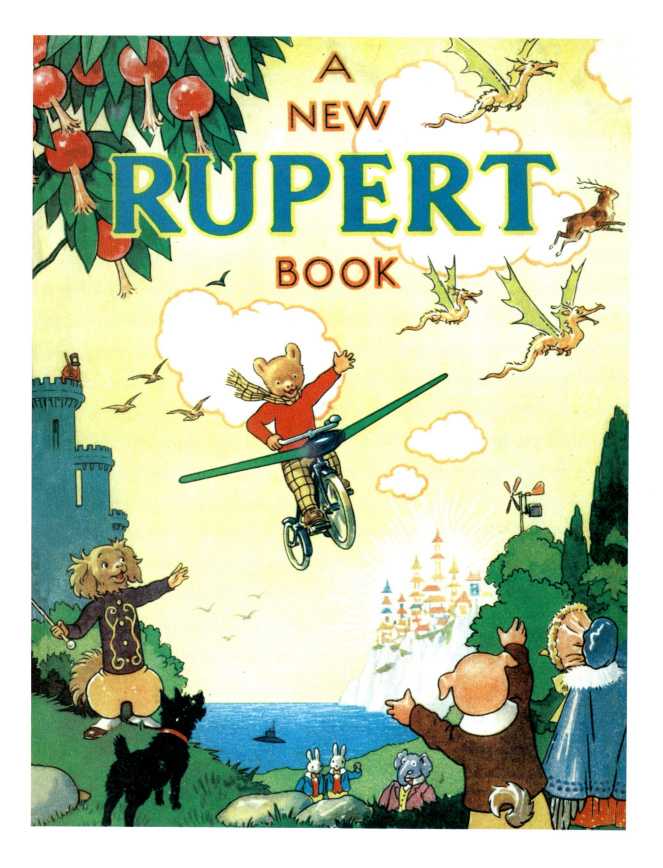

WEEK 11

March

7 Monday

8 Tuesday

Maha Shivaratri

9 Wednesday

10 Thursday

11 Friday

12 Saturday

13 Sunday

Cover of the 1945 annual

March

WEEK 12

14 Monday

Commonwealth Day

15 Tuesday

16 Wednesday

17 Thursday

St Patrick's Day (Eire, N. Ireland)

18 Friday

19 Saturday

20 Sunday

Palm Sunday
Spring Equinox (Japan)

Page 120 of the 1944 annual

March

WEEK 13

21 Monday

Human Rights Day (S. Africa)
Spring Equinox (Japan) (observed)

22 Tuesday

23 Wednesday

Holi

24 Thursday

Maundy Thursday
Jewish Spring Festival (Purim)
Hola Mohalla

25 Friday

Good Friday

26 Saturday

27 Sunday

Easter Sunday
British Summer Time begins

WEEK 14

March/April

28 Monday

Easter Monday
Family Day (S. Africa)

29 Tuesday

30 Wednesday

31 Thursday

1 Friday

2 Saturday

3 Sunday

WEEK 15

April

4 Monday

5 Tuesday

6 Wednesday

7 Thursday

8 Friday

Hindi New Year
Ramayana Week begins

9 Saturday

10 Sunday

1973 endpaper

April

WEEK 16

11 Monday

12 Tuesday

13 Wednesday

14 Thursday

Vaisakhi

15 Friday

Ramanavami

16 Saturday

17 Sunday

Page 119 of the 1950 annual

The old Professor has invited Rupert and Bill Badger to see his new garden. When they arrive they find that he has laid out his paths in a very curious way.

'Come along,' calls the Professor. 'I'll give a bar of chocolate to the first one of you to reach me. You mustn't come across the grass anywhere, and don't walk over the white lines.'

'What fun!' laughs Rupert. 'Let's try. I'll enter on the right and you go to the left.' 'Right-ho,' says Bill.

Which of them wins the bar of chocolate?

1971 endpaper

April

WEEK 17

18 Monday

19 Tuesday

20 Wednesday

21 Thursday

22 Friday

Hanuman Jayanti

23 Saturday

First Day of Passover (Pesach)
St George's Day (England)

24 Sunday

WEEK 18

April/May

25 Monday

Anzac Day (Aus, NZ)

26 Tuesday

27 Wednesday

Freedom Day (S. Africa)

28 Thursday

29 Friday

Showa Day (Japan)

30 Saturday

Last Day of Passover (Pesach)

1 Sunday

Workers' Day (S. Africa)

WEEK 19

May

2 Monday

May Bank Holiday (UK, Eire)
Workers' Day (S. Africa) (observed)

3 Tuesday

Constitution Memorial Day (Japan)

4 Wednesday

Greenery Day (Japan)

5 Thursday

Ascension Day
Children's Day (Japan)

6 Friday

7 Saturday

8 Sunday

Mother's Day (USA, Can, Aus, NZ, S. Africa, Japan)

Page 101 of the 1987 annual

May

WEEK 20

9 Monday

10 Tuesday

11 Wednesday

12 Thursday

13 Friday

14 Saturday

15 Sunday

Whit Sunday (Pentecost)

Page 119 of the 1944 annual

Rupert and his friends are at a moonlight party in Tigerlily's mysterious garden. Suddenly the little Chinese girl waves her wand and all except Rupert disappear. 'Oh dear, they've vanished!' he cries; 'where have they gone?' 'They not go; they still here,' laughs Tigerlily.

(She is quite right. Bill Badger is there, so are Algy Pug, Podgy Pig, Edward Trunk, Willie Whiskers, Rex and Reggie Rabbit and Freddy and Ferdy Fox. Also Tigerlily's two cats. Can you see where they all are?)

May

WEEK 21

16 Monday

17 Tuesday

18 Wednesday

19 Thursday

20 Friday

21 Saturday

22 Sunday

Trinity Sunday

WEEK 22

May

23 Monday

Victoria Day (Can)

24 Tuesday

25 Wednesday

26 Thursday

Corpus Christi

27 Friday

28 Saturday

29 Sunday

WEEK 23 May/June

30 Monday
Spring Bank Holiday (UK)
Memorial Day (USA)

31 Tuesday

1 Wednesday

2 Thursday

Coronation Day

3 Friday

4 Saturday

5 Sunday

Back page of the 1953 adventure series annual

June

WEEK 24

6 Monday

June Bank Holiday (Eire)

7 Tuesday

Ramadan begins

8 Wednesday

9 Thursday

10 Friday

11 Saturday

The Queen's Official Birthday (UK)

12 Sunday

Shavuot begins

Cover of the 1950 annual

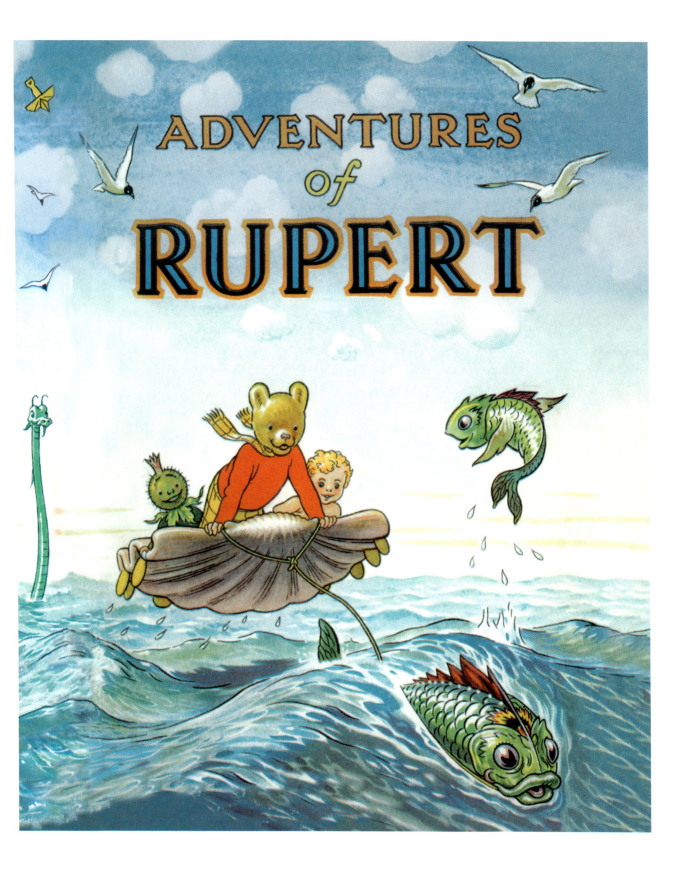

June

WEEK 25

13 Monday

Shavuot ends

14 Tuesday

15 Wednesday

16 Thursday

Youth Day (S. Africa)
Martyrdom of Guru Arjan Dev

17 Friday

18 Saturday

19 Sunday

Father's Day (UK, Eire, USA, Can, S. Africa, Japan)

WEEK 26

June

20 Monday

Summer Solstice

21 Tuesday

22 Wednesday

23 Thursday

24 Friday

25 Saturday

26 Sunday

WEEK 27

June/July

27 Monday

28 Tuesday

29 Wednesday

30 Thursday

1 Friday
Canada Day

2 Saturday

3 Sunday

July

WEEK 28

4 Monday

Independence Day (USA)

5 Tuesday

6 Wednesday

7 Thursday

Ramadan ends

8 Friday

9 Saturday

10 Sunday

Page 119 of the 1947 annual

'Come and have a game of cricket,' says Bill Badger, as he wheels his cycle up to where his pal is sitting. 'Right-o, but I must finish this chapter first,' says Rupert. 'I'll be just five minutes. In the meantime I'll set you a competition. Your name begins with a B. Look around and see if you can find 20 other things beginning with B.'
Can you find the 20 things in five minutes? There are more than 20 in the picture.

July  WEEK 29

11 Monday

12 Tuesday

Battle of the Boyne Day (N. Ireland)

13 Wednesday

14 Thursday

15 Friday

16 Saturday

17 Sunday

WEEK 30

July

18 Monday

Marine Day (Japan)

19 Tuesday

20 Wednesday

21 Thursday

22 Friday

23 Saturday

24 Sunday

WEEK 31   July

_____
                                              25 Monday

_____
                                             26 Tuesday

_____
                                           27 Wednesday

_____
                                            28 Thursday

_____
                                              29 Friday

_____
                                            30 Saturday

_____
                                              31 Sunday

Cover of the 1986 annual

1985 endpaper

August

WEEK 32

1 Monday

Summer Bank Holiday (Scot)
August Bank Holiday (Eire)

2 Tuesday

3 Wednesday

4 Thursday

5 Friday

6 Saturday

7 Sunday

Page 107 of the 1957 annual

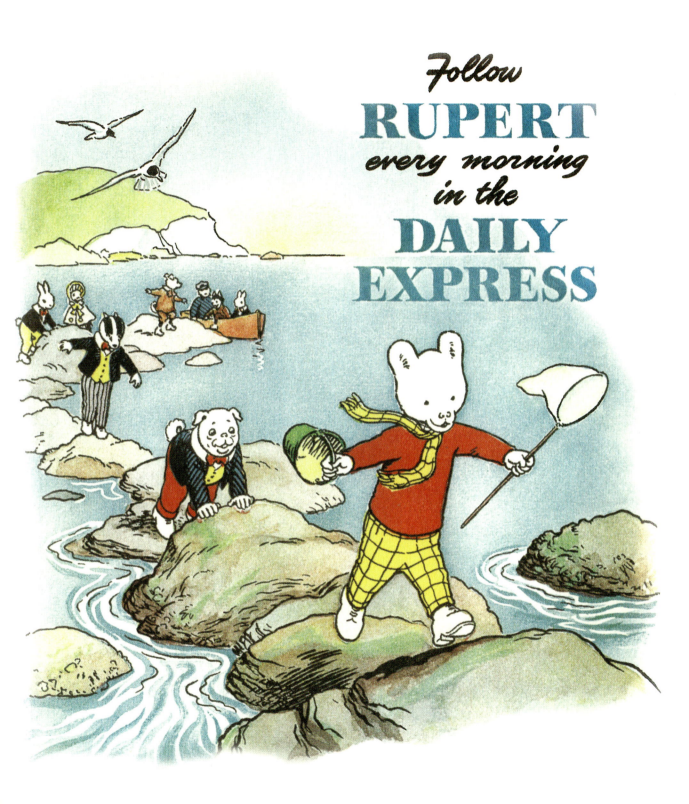

August

WEEK 33

8 Monday

9 Tuesday

National Women's Day (S. Africa)

10 Wednesday

11 Thursday

12 Friday

13 Saturday

14 Sunday

WEEK 34

August

15 Monday

16 Tuesday

17 Wednesday

18 Thursday

Raksha Bandhan

19 Friday

20 Saturday

21 Sunday

WEEK 35

August

---
22 Monday

---
23 Tuesday

---
24 Wednesday

---
25 Thursday

Krishna Janmashthami
---
26 Friday

---
27 Saturday

---
28 Sunday

1976 endpaper

August/September

WEEK 36

29 Monday

Summer Bank Holiday (UK except Scot)

30 Tuesday

31 Wednesday

1 Thursday

2 Friday

3 Saturday

4 Sunday

Father's Day (Aus, NZ)

Cover of the 1944 annual

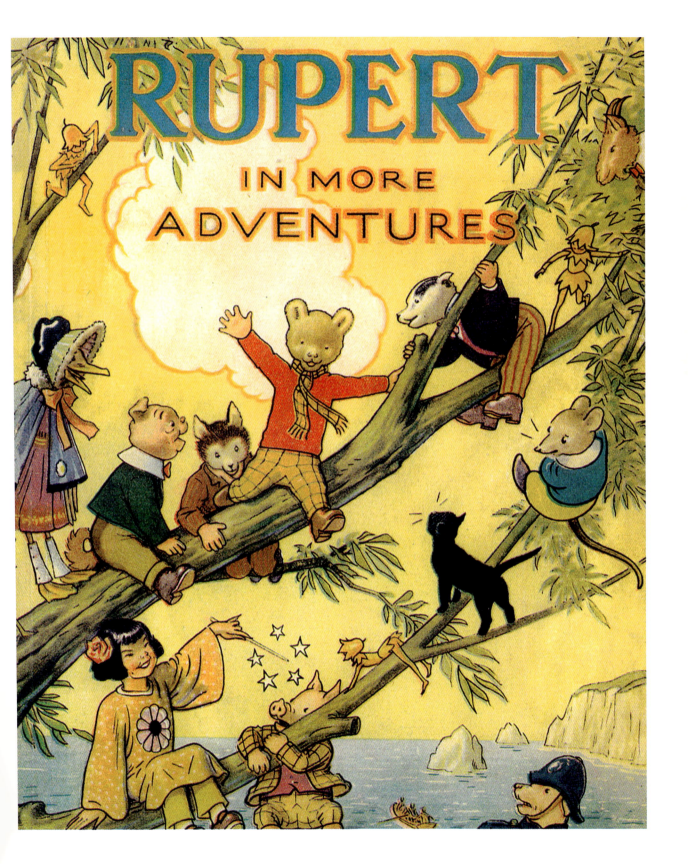

September

WEEK 37

5 Monday

Labour Day (USA, Can)
Ganesh Chaturthi

6 Tuesday

7 Wednesday

8 Thursday

9 Friday

10 Saturday

11 Sunday

Grandparents' Day (USA, Can)

WEEK 38

September

12 Monday

13 Tuesday

14 Wednesday

15 Thursday

16 Friday

17 Saturday

Pitr-paksha begins

18 Sunday

WEEK 39

September

19 Monday

Respect for the Aged Day (Japan)

20 Tuesday

21 Wednesday

International Day of Peace

22 Thursday

Autumn Equinox (Japan)

23 Friday

24 Saturday

Heritage Day (S. Africa)

25 Sunday

Page 115 of the 1975 annual

September/October

WEEK 40

26 Monday

27 Tuesday

28 Wednesday

29 Thursday

30 Friday

Pitr-paksha ends
1 Saturday

Navaratri begins
2 Sunday

Cover of the 2000 annual

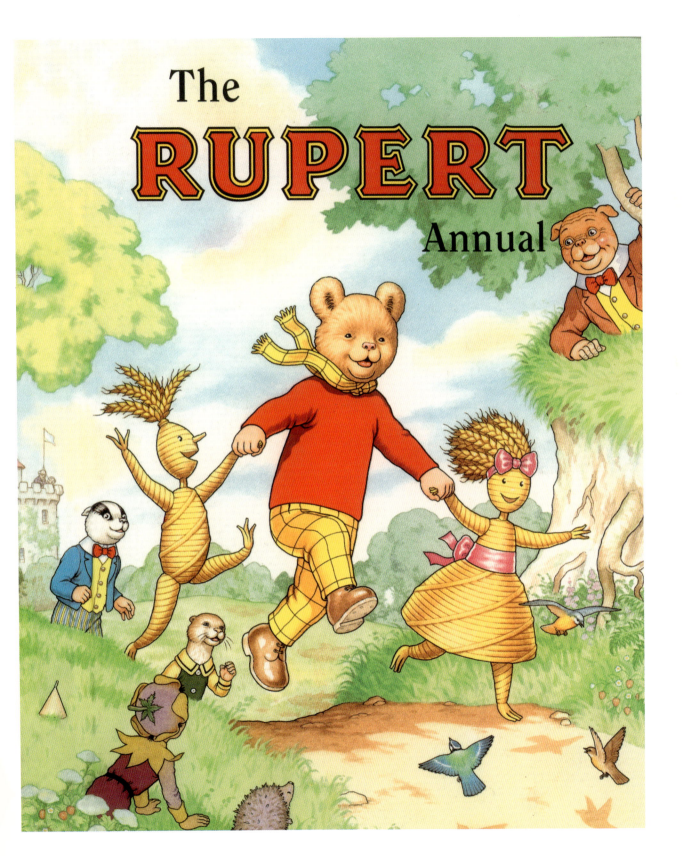

October

WEEK 41

3 Monday

4 Tuesday

Islamic New Year
Jewish New Year (Rosh Hashanah) begins

5 Wednesday

Jewish New Year (Rosh Hashanah) ends

6 Thursday

7 Friday

8 Saturday

9 Sunday

WEEK 42

October

10 Monday

Columbus Day (USA)
Thanksgiving Day (Can)
Health and Sports Day (Japan)

11 Tuesday

Dussehra

12 Wednesday

Day of Atonement (Yom Kippur)

13 Thursday

14 Friday

15 Saturday

16 Sunday

WEEK 43

October

17 Monday

First Day of Tabernacles (Sukkot)

18 Tuesday

Second Day of Tabernacles (Sukkot)

19 Wednesday

20 Thursday

21 Friday

22 Saturday

23 Sunday

Back page of the 1947 adventure series annual

October

WEEK 44

24 Monday

Labour Day (NZ)
Shemini Atzeret

25 Tuesday

Simchat Torah

26 Wednesday

27 Thursday

28 Friday

29 Saturday

30 Sunday

British Summer Time ends
Bandi Chhor Divas
Diwali

WEEK 45

October/November

31 Monday

Hallowe'en
October Bank Holiday (Eire)
Vikram New Year

1 Tuesday

All Saints' Day

2 Wednesday

3 Thursday

National Culture Day (Japan)

4 Friday

5 Saturday

6 Sunday

1986 endpaper

November

WEEK 46

7 Monday

8 Tuesday

9 Wednesday

10 Thursday

11 Friday

Remembrance Day (Armistice Day)
Veterans' Day (USA)

12 Saturday

13 Sunday

Remembrance Sunday

Cover of the 1947 annual

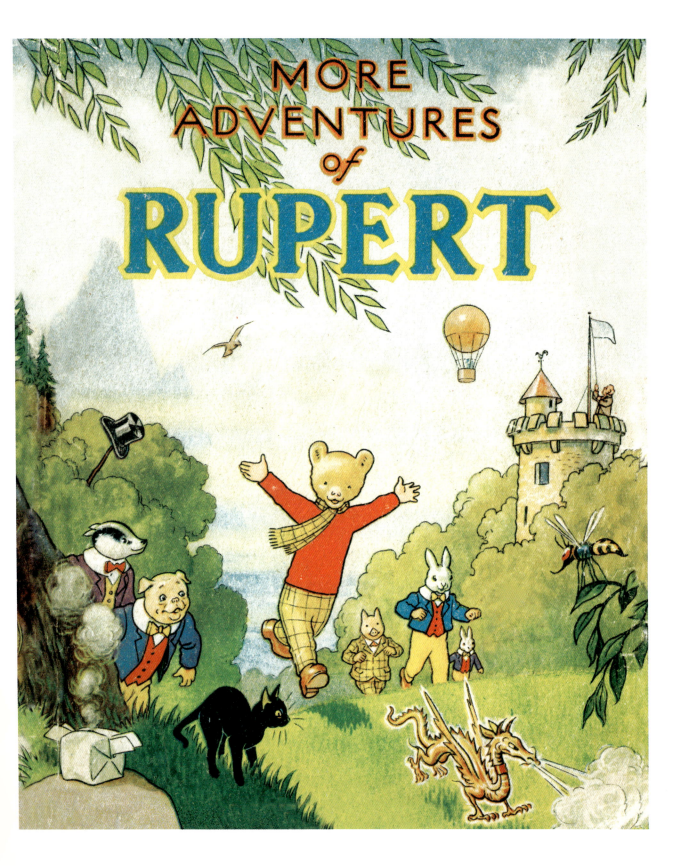

November

WEEK 47

14 Monday

Birthday of Guru Nanak

15 Tuesday

16 Wednesday

17 Thursday

18 Friday

19 Saturday

20 Sunday

WEEK 48

November

21 Monday

22 Tuesday

23 Wednesday

Labour Thanksgiving Day (Japan)

24 Thursday

Martyrdom of Guru Tegh Bahadur
Thanksgiving Day (USA)

25 Friday

26 Saturday

27 Sunday

Advent Sunday

WEEK 49

November/December

28 Monday

29 Tuesday

30 Wednesday

St Andrew's Day (Scot)

1 Thursday

2 Friday

3 Saturday

4 Sunday

Back page of the 1950 adventure series annual

December

WEEK 50

5 Monday

6 Tuesday

7 Wednesday

8 Thursday

9 Friday

10 Saturday

11 Sunday

Cover of the 1953 annual

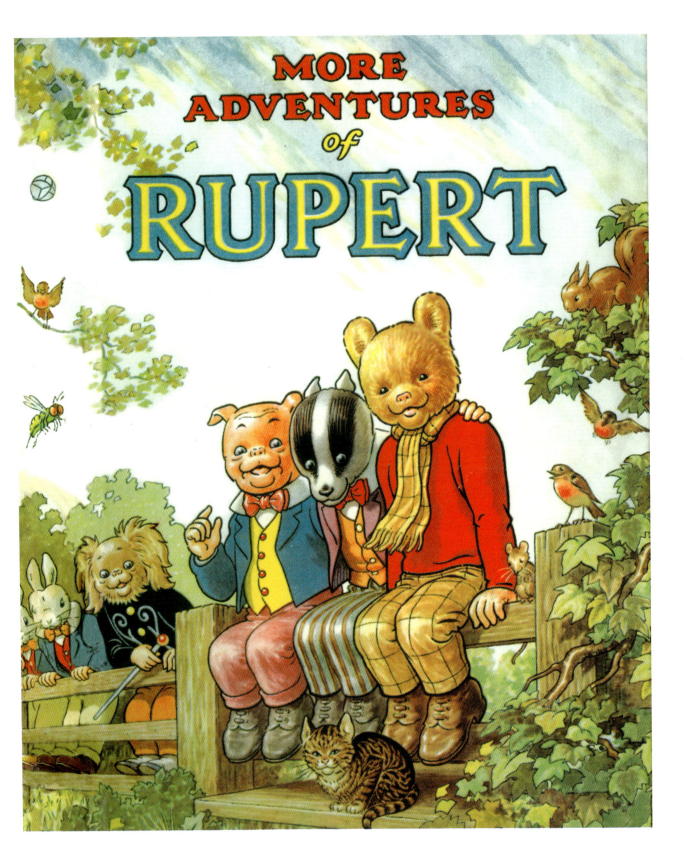

WEEK 51

December

12 Monday

13 Tuesday

14 Wednesday

15 Thursday

16 Friday

Day of Reconciliation (S. Africa)

17 Saturday

18 Sunday

Page 107 of the 1959 annual

December

WEEK 52

19 Monday

20 Tuesday

21 Wednesday

Winter Solstice

22 Thursday

23 Friday

Emperor's Birthday (Japan)

24 Saturday

Christmas Eve

25 Sunday

Christmas Day
Hanukkah begins

Cover of the 1949 annual

WEEK 1

December/January 2017

26 Monday

Public Holiday (UK, Aus, NZ, Can, USA, S. Africa)
Boxing Day
St Stephen's Day (Eire)
Day of Goodwill (S. Africa)

27 Tuesday

Public Holiday (UK, Aus, NZ, Can)

28 Wednesday

29 Thursday

30 Friday

31 Saturday

New Year's Eve

1 Sunday

New Year's Day

1987 endpaper

Cover of the 1962 annual